PSYCHO BUSTERS

5

Story by
Yuya Aoki

Manga by
Akinari Nao

Translated and adapted by
Stephen Paul

Lettered by
North Market Street Graphics

Ballantine Books * New York

Psycho Busters volume 5 is a work of fiction. Names, characters, places, and incidents are the products of the author's imagination or are used fictitiously. Any resemblance to actual events, locales, or persons, living or dead, is entirely coincidental.

A Del Rey Manga/Kodansha Trade Paperback Original

Published in the United States by Del Rey, an imprint of The Random House Publishing Group, a division of Random House, Inc., New York.

Publication rights arranged through Kodansha Ltd.

First published in Japan in 2008 by Kodansha Ltd., Tokyo

ISBN 978-0-345-51037-2

Printed in the United States of America

www.delreymanga.com

9 8 7 6 5 4 3 2 1

Translator/adapter: Stephen Paul
Lettering: North Market Street Graphics

Contents

Honorifics Explained

Throughout the Del Rey Manga books, you will find Japanese honorifics left intact in the translations. For those not familiar with how the Japanese use honorifics and, more important, how they differ from American honorifics, we present this brief overview.

Politeness has always been a critical facet of Japanese culture. Ever since the feudal era, when Japan was a highly stratified society, use of honorifics—which can be defined as polite speech that indicates relationship or status—has played an essential role in the Japanese language. When addressing someone in Japanese, an honorific usually takes the form of a suffix attached to one's name (example: "Asuna-san"), is used as a title at the end of one's name, or appears in place of the name itself (example: "Negi-sensei," or simply "Sensei!").

Honorifics can be expressions of respect or endearment. In the context of manga and anime, honorifics give insight into the nature of the relationship between characters. Many English translations leave out these important honorifics and therefore distort the feel of the original Japanese. Because Japanese honorifics contain nuances that English honorifics lack, it is our policy at Del Rey not to translate them. Here, instead, is a guide to some of the honorifics you may encounter in Del Rey Manga.

-san: This is the most common honorific and is equivalent to Mr., Miss, Ms., or Mrs. It is the all-purpose honorific and can be used in any situation where politeness is required.

-sama: This is one level higher than "-san" and is used to confer great respect.

-dono: This comes from the word "tono," which means "lord." It is an even higher level than "-sama" and confers utmost respect.

-kun: This suffix is used at the end of boys' names to express familiarity or endearment. It is also sometimes used by men among friends, or when addressing someone younger or of a lower station.

-chan: This is used to express endearment, mostly toward girls. It is also used for little boys, pets, and even among lovers. It gives a sense of childish cuteness.

Bozu: This is an informal way to refer to a boy, similar to the English terms "kid" and "squirt."

Sempai/ Senpai: This title suggests that the addressee is one's senior in a group or organization. It is most often used in a school setting, where underclassmen refer to their upperclassmen as "sempai." It can also be used in the workplace, such as when a newer employee addresses an employee who has seniority in the company.

Kohai: This is the opposite of "sempai" and is used toward underclassmen in school or newcomers in the workplace. It connotes that the addressee is of a lower station.

Sensei: Literally meaning "one who has come before," this title is used for teachers, doctors, or masters of any profession or art.

[blank]: This is usually forgotten in these lists, but it is perhaps the most significant difference between Japanese and English. The lack of honorific means that the speaker has permission to address the person in a very intimate way. Usually, only family, spouses, or very close friends have this kind of permission. Known as *yobisute,* it can be gratifying when someone who has earned the intimacy starts to call one by one's name without an honorific. But when that intimacy hasn't been earned, it can be very insulting.

Psycho Busters
5
Story by Yuya Aoki,
Manga by Akinari Nao

Stories

The Story So Far

One day during summer vacation, boring middle-schooler Kakeru Hase met Ayano, a pretty girl with ESP. She and her friends Jôi, Kaito and Xiao Long are all escapees from the "Greenhouse," a sinister laboratory that raises psychic soldiers through inhumane means—and the Greenhouse will do anything to get them back! When he helps his new friends evade capture, Kakeru is drawn into an all-out war between psychic forces!

When summer vacation is over, Ayano and her friends join Kakeru's school, along with several clandestine members of the Greenhouse. One of these enemies, Kiryû, kidnaps Ayano and *kills* her! Kakeru explodes with rage at this unthinkable sight, and his mind jumps to a "crack in time," where he meets a mysterious girl known as Tomoe. It is here that he learns he has the ability to rewind time, which he then uses to defeat Kiryû and bring Ayano back to life!

Cast of Characters

Ayano

Ability: Astral Projection

A girl who is attracted to Kakeru. His meeting with her was what dragged Kakeru into the battle they now face.

Jôi

Ability: Foresight

The leader of the five, always cool-headed and rational.

Kakeru Hase

Ability: Dimensional Barrier Generation (Time Manipulation)

A boy whose powers are so great, the fate of the world rests in his hands.

Xiao Long

Ability: Qigong and Healing

A quiet, kindhearted boy. Good at cooking and kung fu.

Kaito

Ability: Firestarting

A rough-and-tumble dude found leading a pack of street thugs in Yokohama's Nationless Quarter.

PARTNER

ENEMY

Ikushima

Acting chief of the psychic-raising laboratory, the "Greenhouse." A dangerous man who plots to use Kakeru's powers to his own ends.

Todoroki

Ability: ?

A psychic under Ikushima's command.

Fuyuko

Ability: Materialization of Vengeful Spirits

A psychic under Ikushima's command. Was previously beaten by Kakeru's group, against which she now holds a grudge.

Tomoe

A girl that Kakeru met in the crack in time.

Hiyama

An employee at Kakeru's school. Secretly a member of the "Crimers," a group that hunts down psychics.

Shô

Ability: Teleportation

A psychic working for Ikushima. Attending the same school as Kakeru and his friends.

Takemaru

Ability: Psychoki

Was once working Ikushima, but afte battle with Kakeru, he just might be considered a friend.

Poss
Partn

Maya (Mamidori):

Ability: Illusions

Formerly Ikushima's pawn, until Kakeru saved her life. She spends most of her time living as Mamidori, using her illusory powers.

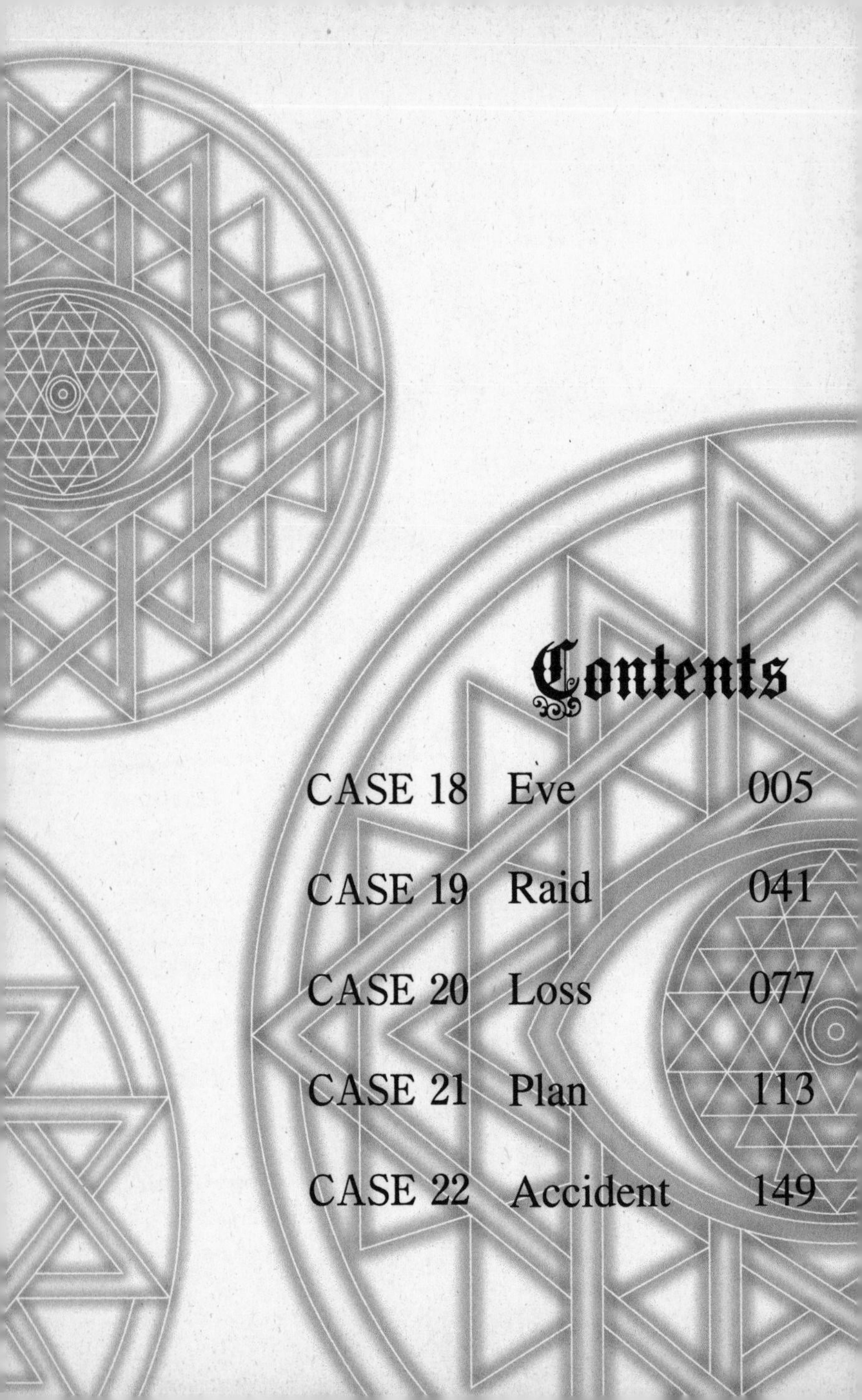

Contents

But *why*, Chief?
Why am I being removed from duty?!

I cannot accept this treat-ment!
All your recent efforts have resulted in failure.
If you are not brought to heel, the world will learn of our existence.

B-but, Chief...
You need to cool it, Izanami.

Case 18 – Eve

I am assigning you a new mission.
What is this?
Monitor that boy.
If you should detect any suspicious activity, you may terminate him, if necessary.

Oh yeah?
Mind repeating that for me one more time?
What?
Sure thing! As many times as it takes!

I told you! Okonomiyaki is meant to be eaten with rice! It takes the place of a side dish! Don't you get it?! You know why okonomiyaki sauce is so thick? So it goes perfectly with a serving of white rice! It's supposed to be like eating sobameshi! Just think of that sauce, mixed with mayonnaise, and then—
Hah! I don't have to eat it to know what I'm talking about! Okonomiyaki is served over rice? That's crazy! Okonomiyaki batter is made with flour! Flour and rice are both carbohydrates, so why would you eat the both of them together?! Okonomiyaki is its own dish and works perfectly by itself! There's no need to add a single grain of rice to it; all that will do is detract from the—

Looks like we've still got a score to settle, then!
Oh yeah? I'll blast you to smithereens!
...
They're fighting again... Those two will never be friends.
YAWWWN
Hey! Kakeru, you ought to eat your eggplant!

Say that *after* you try it!
Why would I need to *try* it?
Huh? Aww, okay...
You shouldn't be picky! It's not healthy.
Y-yeah, I know...
What's wrong with that? I don't see why you should force yourself to eat some-thing you hate!
Aaah! Mamidori-san!
Get off of him.
Look at my lunch! I think I made more than I can eat... Will you help?
Stop that!
He has to finish eating his own, first.
Here, Kakeru.
SHWIP

Why? *Mine* is handmade, *and* it tastes better. Don't you agree?
That one was made by Xiao Long-kun, wasn't it?
Besides, what makes it that much of your business, Ayano-chan?

I mean, it's not like you're *going out* or anything, right?
Huh...?
When you say "going out"...
...You're talking about... umm, you know...

Well, of *course* we're not!
That's disgusting!
CRIKK
HEH
HEH

DINNNG DONNNG
Huh? Lunch is over already?
Man, I'm tired...
What's up, Ayano?
That's funny...
Look!
Well, you shouldn't have bought such a cheap watch, then.
How rude! My watch is *not* cheap!
My watch is five minutes behind...
It's one of those electronically aligned watches that only loses a single second in 100,000 years.
Some-thing's not right...

Well, the bell is what counts here, so let's get going before we're late to class.
Okay...
Her watch is behind...

The time is late. Could that mean...?
...But no. That's too much of a time slip.

Kakeru's power might be great, but he can't have used it more than a handful of times.
It would mean that his abilities are so extreme, they're even...
Jôi...?
!!
They're coming.
BOOM
!!
What's going on?!

DMM
ZSHH

DOOM

W-who *are* these guys? Are they the Farmers?
No...even worse, I'm afraid.

I know these people.
They're with Hiyama-san...

Something tells me they're not here to make friends.
No, I don't think so.

SHWUP

!!
My knife...
FZSHHH
Heh heh...
You can't put a mark on me with one of those dinky things.

SHHHH
Hah!!
DOMM

W-what's wrong?!
CHKK
TWIK
Aaah!!
DATTA
DATTA
What are you doing?!
We're on your side!
DATTA
Piece of cake!
Possession complete. ♡
FWH
GSHHH
Krrr!!

Don't waste your time.
If I know exactly where and when you're going to attack...
TAP
...You don't stand a chance at stopping me.
FWOPP
Ayano, someone's aiming at us from above! Stop him!
Kaito, there are two people coming from the right at the same time!
I'm on it!
Roger that!

!!
BWOOM
What the—?!
Aaah!
I can't get out!
What a joke!
I'll just burn through this net in a...
...Huh?
What's wrong, Kaito?!

...I can't make any fire...
What?
Hey! I can't use my powers, either!
I can't shoot qigong...
This must be...
...An anti-psychic weapon!!
Quick on the uptake, I see...
This is an anti-psychic net, made from very special materials.
It limits the psychic abilities of anyone caught underneath it.
Even the most dangerous psychic is nothing more than just another child when caught in its snares.

Hey!
There's a chick in here!
Huh?
Actually, she's pretty cute!
Hey, knock it off!
Yaaa!!
Ayano?!
Remember when you got in trouble for doing this, the other time?!
Who cares? No one's going to find out!

Knock it off!
Oh, shut up and stay out of this!
Grr...
VMMM
Man, she's *stacked* for a middle schooler!
I guess some psychics even come *hotter* than regular humans.
Stop it!!

Get your hands off of Ayano!!
GWOHH
!!
Kakeru, *no!!*
Jôi?
B-but *why*...?
What did I tell you? You shouldn't use your power at every opportunity.
......
B-but...
Even under these cir-cumstances, he was able to deploy his powers! I was right—he is absurdly powerful.
But that's what makes it even *more* imperative that he *doesn't* go wild!!

What's the big problem? I'm just gonna see the difference between her body and a human body! It's *research*, see?
That's not what we're here to do, and you know it!!
ZSHH
Huh?
Aaaaahh!!
Holes! I'm all fulla holes!!
Oh God, help meee!
SHH
Wha...?

Hiyama-san!
たじっ
HURR
Izanami! W-what are *you* doing *here*?!
T-this is crazy! You're not supposed to...
Am I not allowed to be here?
But...the psychics are your enemies, remember?!
That might be so, but *these* people are my friends.
I'm not going to stand by and watch them die!

D-don't you understand?! We've been given orders to kill you on sight!
The only reward for a traitor who protects psychics is death!
You won't leave this spot ali...
I'd like to see you try.
DOKK
Wha...?
I want to see you *try* to stop me.
Agh...

Y-you're going to regret this!
BZMM
You won't get off, next time!

They're gone...
Are we safe, then?
I think so.

ZSHH

Hiyama-san!!
HUFF
HUFF
Are you hurt?!

FACULTY ROOM
......
Mm...
Are you awake?
Hah...
What is it?
I was just remembering when something like this happened before.
Jôi...
I had Xiao Long take care of your wounds. Everyone else is back home.
...Now, tell me everything.

......
Remember earlier, when you called me a "spy"?
...Yes?
I'm in the Police Department's Unofficial Crisis Management and Erasers Agency, "Crimers."
Our duty is to wipe out the psychic-raising agency called the "Farm."
Yesterday, we raided their facility, code-named "Greenhouse."
Move in!!
DA
DA
DA
DA
Don't let a single rat escape this place alive!!
But all of their executives had already been murdered, by a man named Ikushima.
BLAM
Our unit was entirely wiped out by Ikushima and another psychic. I was the only survivor.
Faced with a sea change in th momentum of power, Crimers was forced to make the decisio to destroy a young man heavil connected to this series of events.
Kakeru...
Correct.
But Hiyama-san, that would mean you were supposed to kill Kakeru just now...
......
......
I might have grown...too attached to him.

He's just like my late younger brother.
My brother was sickly, missed school often, and was a regular target for bullies.
I told him, "A real man fights back!"
But he just laughed it off.
He always said he could never stand the thought of hurting another person.
When he died...I knew he didn't have much longer, but it was still a terrible shock.
I failed several missions, and was given a different assign-ment.
Pssh...
You want me to babysit some kid?
Monitor Kakeru Hase, Category Zero.

...This is him.
Sheesh, look at him. He's been singled out for harassment on the very first day of school!
And this kid's supposed to be dangerous enough to need monitoring?!
Here.
Uh... thanks...
I see... But you realize that if you don't change your-self, that kind of bullying will never stop, don't you?
Have some confidence! You can program fun computer games, can't you?
Besides, haven't you ever wanted to be tough enough that you could fight off those bullies?!
You're pathetic!
Heh heh...

Well, if there are people who hurt others, that means there are people who are hurt, right?
I'm on the side that gets hurt, already. I wouldn't want to make any more of us.
"Well, if you're hurting people, that means other people are being hurt."
"I'd rather be the kind that *gets* hurt."

And ever since then...
Against my better judgment, I've been giving him advice and helping him out.

I had always hoped, "As long as nothing happens..."
...But my weakness has led to the worst possible outcome.

I've been lying to Kakeru all this time.
And I called myself a friend. I'm a terrible person.

......

But to-day was different.
SHH
Huh...?

Would you like to go look at the stars?
You might find that something good will come of it, tonight.

....
Is that...?
Kakeru...

Oh...
Hiyama-san!!
TMM
TMM
Are you well enough to walk?!
Y-yeah...

Kakeru... I...
I have something I'd like to say to you...

K-Kakeru...
I just want you to know...
....

Thank you, Hiyama-san.
Kakeru...
I've been thinking about things between you and me.
Remember how you cheered me up, the very first time we met?
Ever since then, you've been watching out for me.
Huh...?

You said you liked the games I programmed.
You stayed up all night trying to beat them.
That made me really happy to know.
It helped me cope with coming to school.
I knew that I wasn't all alone there...
You were always a friend to me.
And thanks to that, I was able to meet Jôi and all my other *new* friends.
Kakeru...
I have a lot to thank you for, no matter *what* you are.
I still love you, Hiyama-san.

Wha...? Uh, Hiyama-san...?
Y-you're kind of... hurting me...
......
Thanks...
You little dummy...
......
No prob...

Well, things are about to get busy.
Now we're going to have to fight off *two* forces at once: Crimers *and* Ikushima.

The real war is yet to come.

……
Real... war...?
He's right...
But I'll be here to protect Kakeru...

That's what...
...I swore to do...

(I've never ridden on a bus by myself, before. I'm really nervous!)

(Those other kids are having fun... I wonder if they'll let me join them.)

Case 19 – Raid

"Do you mind if I sit here?"

(She's cute!!)

"N-not at all."

"Your name's Kakeru? I'm all by myself, too. Let's be friends!"

SQUEEZE
"My name's Tomoe. Nice to meet you, Kakeru-chan."
NOD
NOD
MUYO

"Unng...
W-what
happened...?"

"Oh!
Tomoe-chan!
Where's
Tomoe-chan?!"

Aaaaahhh!!

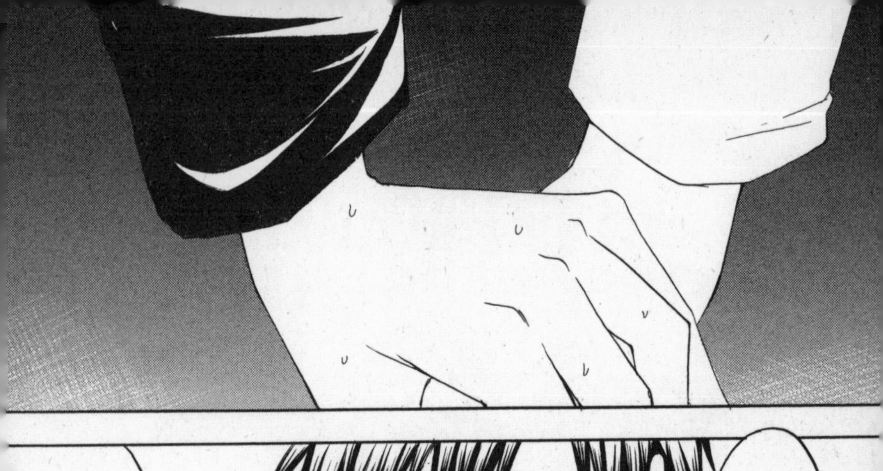

....
Are you sure you're all right, Ayano?

Yes... I just didn't think my car sickness would be this bad.
Let me just sit here and hold onto your hand...

We didn't *have* to take the bus, you know...
I know, but it's my first time. I always want to try something new at least *once*.

Want to get off and take a break?
No, we're almost there. I'll manage.

Besides, it's our first time out in a while. I don't want to ruin it.

We're here!
秋葉原駅
Come on, Kakeru, let's go!
AKIHABARA STATION
A date alone with Ayano. This is the best day ever!
And I already got to hold her hand! I can feel good things coming today!!

Yesterday
You're going out? Well, I'm not joining you.
I just got my hands on this new game; it's supposed to be really good.
Xiao Long and I are gonna play it on Sunday.
Man, that's gonna be fun!
I think I'll decline, as well.
I've got something to take care of.
You two enjoy yourselves.
Aww... So neither Kaito, Xiao Long, *nor* Jôi can come?
I guess it'll just be you and me tomor-row, then.
I know where I'd like to go...

But why did she pick Akiba, of all places?
I mean, in a way, it's home territory for *me*, but I can't imagine what Ayano would find enjoyable about the place...

W-what should I do? How can I make this work?
Think, Kakeru, think. Use your brain to its fullest extent, and you'll find an answer.

The computer parts shop.
No... Ayano will find that boring.
I sure love it, though!

The game store!
No... There are game stores closer to home with the same stuff.

Besides, how is this at all like a date...?
Huh? Ayano?
Kakeru!!

Here! Over here!!
Uh...
Ayano... san?
Where'd you get that outfit?
Some people at that café over there said they want me to work for them.

What do you think?
Does it look good on me?

Y-yes... Of course! But...
Look, over there! It's an undiscovered new under-ground idol!

ZMM
Excuse me, miss! May I take a photo-graph?
ZMM
Huh?! What?!
Let's go give that outfit back!!
Uh... okay!

CHAIRWOMAN

I'm tired, but that was a lot of fun!
What I like about this place is all the different things you can see!
That's very true.
Like, I didn't know you could buy *oden* in a can.
Uhh... I think you're missing the point.

Say, Ayano...
Hmm?
Why did you want to hang out in Akiba?
You could have said lots of other places...like an amusement park, for instance.

You're right...
But the first time we took a trip together, I wanted to come here.

You like this place, don't you?
Huh?!

H...h-h-how...how did you know? Did you use your telepathy to...
No! I wouldn't use it for something like that!

...I just remember something you said before.
That you liked to come here to buy computer parts and games and stuff...

I wanted to start off by going somewhere you really liked.
Ayano...
She put all that thought into it...
I-I-I...
I had a lot of fun, too. I don't know if I've ever had such a great time.
So...
Well...

GRRG
I have to tell her, today.

Things got all mixed up last time...
Not on your life!!

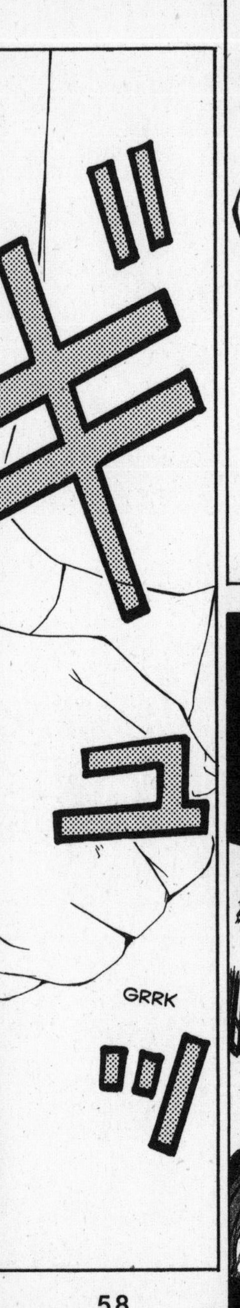
GRRK

Ayano!!
Wha...?

I just want to say that...

I love you!!
I want you!!
I...I do, too...
I feel the same way about you, Kaito-kun...
BA-BUMP
BA-BUMP
But I just can't do it!
WHACK
Dangit! Why not?!
Geez, why can't I get her to fall in love with me?!
Is it because I didn't follow up with her request to walk home the other day?!
I'm gonna get a "just friends" ending!

Man, now I wish I had just gone with Kakeru and Ayano.
What do you think, Xiao Long?
......
Xiao Long?
!!
SHH
Whoa!!
BOOOM
W-what was that?!
KSHHNK

Roaaaaarr!!

!!
Wha...?

Aaaahhh!!
It's a monster!!
Breaking news!! Giant, unidentified creatures...
Mysterious Creatures Appear All Over Japan!!
...Have just been spotted at several locations all throughout Japan!!

ROHHHHH
YRAHHH
DMM

Giants! Not again! But why...?
Let's go, Xiao Long!
Did you get a hold of Jôi?
No, I can't reach him.
This is different from the way it's been before!
I sure hope Kakeru, Ayano and Jôi are okay...

Sheesh...

You just *had* to tag along with me, and what do I get for indulging you? *This!*

I didn't expect to see *you* in the flesh.
You must be getting desperate.

HEH
Please. I'd prefer that you call me "well-prepared."

I *am* a perfec- tionist, after all.
POIK

I simply made the choice that offered me the best chance to meet my goals...
...Jôi Toma- kun.

......
I should have known I couldn't keep my identity a secret.
Of course you can't.
Not when it comes to *you*.

Then that makes things simple!
...Just the thought of having the same blood as you running in my veins makes me sick.
What are they saying?

I can kill you right here and now, and sever the strings of eternity.
You won't be laying a finger on Kakeru!!
HEH
What's so funny?
......
Oh...
I was just wondering what our Category Zero friend was up to at this moment.

Is there an assassin heading for Kakeru as we speak...?
But with Kakeru in control of his abilities now...he should be able to fend for himself.
......
...Kakeru will be fine, you say?
What...?
What did I just tell you?
I'm a perfectionist—an obsessive planner.
The Category Zero—the "Chronodiver"—might control time, but he is not invincible.
There are numerous means by which he can be overcome.
What?!

You don't mean...
You woke *him* up, didn't you?
Yes.
Our *other* Category Zero.

Urrg... gh...
Aa... aah...

洗濯機
テレビ DVD デジカメ・コンポ
Pao
コノアフ

W-why...?

Why don't...my powers work?!

More...
BOOOM
GRKK
DMMMMM
More...
Hee hee hee!
More destruction! I must have more!!

Case 20 – Loss

Wait just a second!!
What the hell do you think you're doing?! Is this another one of Ikushima's orders?!
Orders? Orders have nothing to do with it...
I've been waiting.
Huh...?
My Gi-kun is gone... All you see now are fakes.
Xiao Long! Kakeru Hase!
You will *pay* for the crime of stealing my dear Gi-kun away from me!

ヒュウウウ
SWSHHH
ROHHHHH
Don't waste your time!
That thing doesn't stand a chance against Xiao Long's qigong!

That might be true...
But...

ZLOOM
What if there are *many* of them?
Wha...?
Where are they all *coming* from?

This is crazy...
When did she learn to control so many at once?

Was Jôi right?
Did she power-up too, after meeting Kakeru?

DA-DOOM

BWOOM

More and more keep coming! There's no *end* to them!
Isn't there anything you can do, Xiao Long?!

No...
HUFF
HUFF
Against *this* many...

I'm helpless.
DMMM

We're gonna die!!

What the...? I'm fine!
If you're having *that* much trouble with an enemy like *this*, maybe you're just losing your grip.
Yeah, really. Is this all you "wild-types" amount to?
Huh?!
On the other hand, I guess I should thank you for giving me the chance to make this uber-cool entrance.
Wh...
Why?!

I-it's *you* people! How come you're-?!
!!
You don't think this kind of mess means trouble for us, too?
She's taken this a bit too far. Someone needs a *spanking*.
Plus, I'm bored!!
BOOM

I mean, don't get the wrong idea or any-thing. We're not here to save you.
But we're also not going to sit back and watch you bungle this thing up.
Plus, we don't want you making us look bad. We lost to you last time out, remember?
HMPH
Whatever you say.
Just come out and say you want a rematch with me!!
Why don't you just be honest?
What?
BAM
Hah! Save the crazy talk for the asylum!!

DBOOMM

N-no...
All of my giants, gone in an instant...
So...
It's just you that's left, huh?
......
DRIP
Why...?
DRIP
Why is it always just me?!
Why am I always left out?!
Is it that bad that my powers are weak?!
Is it that creepy that my ability is to give form to angry spirits?!
GWAHH
Well, *all* psychics should be that creepy!!

What do you want us to do, then?
You're knocking down the town becaus you're sulking about being alone.
Is that going to make you happy?
I...
I just...

Why would anyone care about the differences in our powers? That's stupid.
If that was the case, I'd never speak a *word* to this fool!

The problem is that you're shunning everyone else and using that to feel persecuted and alone.

These things might be your friends...but at their root, they're still evil spirits.
If you want to help them, you have to find a way to solve their earthly problems and send them to the afterlife.
Be quiet!
They're my only friends!
I know someone who would ask to be your friend, even if you were already his enemy...
What...
Oh, I do, too!
Ugh, he's such a pain in the neck...
That's right...
He's pretty weird...
He's a fool who actually thinks that he can find mutual understanding with *anyone*, no matter who they are.

See?
You're not alone anymore.
Wha...?

……
Okay...
FWOOO
Thank you, Gi-kun...
I've finally... made friends.

So, Todoroki's the name of this psychic that Kakeru's dealing with now?
Ehh, I bet Kakeru will be fine.
What's his power?
I don't know.
Between this guy and Kiryû, we don't know anything about these psychics...
You've never met him?

I've met him...
Only once...
He was scary.
I was nothing, compared to him.
In his eyes, you could see real hatred of the entire world.

HOBBY
SEGA
ONIJYU MARU
BRRM
Gosh, there sure are a lot of people here.
Yeah. Well, it's a Sunday...
BRRM
D-do you think we should leave, now?
Y-yeah...
Wait, Kakeru! Look!!
What...?

Electronics
paox.co.jp
Whoa!
Isn't that...?
paox
Why is that giant on the...?
I don't know, but it could mean the others are in danger!

BFF
Sorry.
It's okay.
My fault for not watching.
We have to hurry and get in touch with...
ZKK

What...? All those people... gone?!
Does that mean what I think it does?

Enemy psychics.
Be careful, Ayano!!
冷暖 エアコン
人気ソフト大展示
ポケット
GPP
Huh?
Well, well... Enjoying a date, are we?
Kakeru!!
What does he think he's...
Hmm...
I see.
......

How *dare* you speak to me that way!

Who *are* you, any-way?!

...I like you.
くるっ
SPIN
FMM
I want to make you mine... by force!!

Huh...
DROOP
Ohh...

DLOP
Oopsy.
What did you do to Ayano?!
Powers activated...

SWOO
!!

But, no...!!
DMM

I acti-vated my powers...
DGKK
How come he's still moving?!

You shouldn't use your power at every opportunity.

Why should I care?
ZAP

If I don't use it *now*, I'm a failure of a man!!
KREEEE

Okay, I've rewound time.
Now I can keep Ayano away from...

Ayano!!
Huh...?
She disapp...
GOKK

Urgh.
Oofh!!
THDD
Again!!
One more time!
DMM
Why...?
Why aren't my powers activat-ing?!
GROKK

......
Heh heh...
What is this...?
Are you really *the* Kakeru Hase?
You swear you're not some look-alike imposter?
You're *weak!*
You're *beyond* weak!!
Is this all you amount to?!
Ha ha ha!!
......

Hah...
I finally...
I finally met you... for *this*?
W...
Wait...
Ayano...
Put... Ayano... down...

We're not done yet...
I promised to protect her...

!!
Aha...

It looks like... there's just a slight change in plans.
What?!

Todoroki, you idiot...
Didn't I tell you capture the Category Zero?
Well, he's only a copy, after all.
No matter. This will hardly ruin my overall plan.

As a matter of fact, Jôi, I did not come here today to chat with *you*. I came to meet the charming lady you are keeping company.
Me?!
Yes.
I've come scouting, as a matter of fact.
Despite being entirely unrelated, you have a very deep bond with Kakeru Hase, the Category Zero.
I will need you, in order to manipulate him.
Oh, no you don't!
I'm not putting Kakeru in *your* hands!

...Is that so?
I suppose we'll have to leave at that. This time.
!!
FFH
He... vanished...
....
Kakeru!!

......
HUFF
HUFF
Finally...
When I had... *finally* managed to...
コクッ
NOD

Finally managed to tell her...
...How I feel...

I'm so powerless.

And I...
...love you, too, Kakeru.
I'll admit...
Whaaaaa?!
SLOOP
I didn't think you were much help, at first.
But you did your best for me.
And when it really mattered, you were there to save me.
Will you promise to keep watching over me?

TKK
TKK
Wait...
Who are you?
Why are you crying?

HUFF
HUFF
HUFF

W- where am I...?
The... school...?
So...
So I failed...
I didn't protect her.

SCIENCE CLASS
I wasn't expecting Kakeru to go down like that.
Is this "Todoroki" guy another psychic from the Greenhouse?

If he was, we would know him.
But could a Category Four nobody turn into a Category One overnight?
No way. A flea doesn't turn into a wolf in just a few days.
Well, what's going on, then?! We need to act fast. I'm worried about Ayano...

Either way, we're gonna have to deal with Todoroki somehow.
Yeah...

When we found Kakeru wiped out on the ground...
...He was speaking while half conscious.
He said his "powers were useless."
THDD
Oofh!!
As if everything he did was manipulated against him by the enemy.
Wait a minute...
That sounds...
Exactly like what happened when Kakeru beat us...
Raaagh!!
CRACK
BOINK
BWOOOOSH
Huh?
KRISHHK
BOINK

My theory is this...
Todoroki and Kakeru have the *same* power!
B-but...
I thought there was only *one* Category Zero!

I did hear a few stories when we were still at the Greenhouse...
Stories about psychics who were neither wild types, nor cultivated-types.
As I'm sure you all know, at the Greenhouse we were separated into two categories: wild and cultivated.
Cultivated
Fuyuko
Takemaru
Shô
Maya
Psychics whose powers were developed and honed through the administration of special drugs
Wild
Jôi
Ayano
Xiao Long
Kaito
Natural psychics who awakened to their latent abilities after some point or event.
But what if there were people who *didn't* fit in either group?
What do you mean, Jôi?
I mean, what if there were people who had their powers from the very start?
You mean...
Exactly.

People who were bred specifically to be psychics...
What if they used all the data they collected from us...

...to create the perfect psychic, entirely from scratch?

But...
That's crazy...
And if true, nearly unstoppable...
I can't think of how to beat him...
DSHH
!?
What was that sound?!
!!
Kakeru!!
HUFF
HUFF

What are you doing, Kakeru?!
You aren't well enough to be walking around yet!
Ha ha... I have to go... Ayano...
Ayano... needs me...
No, what you need now is *rest!*
You can't do anything in that condition!
First we need to think of *how* to beat him!

C'mon, Kakeru, this is crazy.
Jôi's right; rest comes first.

But I still have to go!!

Ayano's in danger...!
Kakeru.

DOKK
Kaito!!
ZSHHH

......
Did that knock some sense into you, Kakeru?
Kaito...

Follow Jôi's orders, for now.
ZWIP
Or this time, you're only going to get yourself slaughtered.
......
If you still want to go *right now*, then prove you're capable!
HRP
Beat me down, right here and now!
If you're going to beat Todoroki, you should be able to manage *that* easily!

What are you going to accomplish by dying now?
Remember what we saw? The image of the world, destroyed...
You're the only one who can stop it.
You're supposed to save the world, *remember?!*

Ha... ha ha.
Me...? Save the world?
You don't *really*...
...think I have the power to do that, do you?

Wh...
What... did... you... say?
And I'm not going to go beat him. I already lost...
When I was little...I wanted to be a hero.
A big strong guy with special powers who could help everyone.
But...
I'm not! I can't do *anything!!*
And I still *have to go!!*

ガッ
GRAK
Stop it, Kaito!
I'm honestly disgusted! I thought you were better than that... I really did.
Well, fine! Have fun doing what-ever you think you're doing!
ぼそっ
PSSH
What-ever. I'm just a...
Hey!
TRUDGE
ズリ
TRUDGE
W- wait a minute!
There he goes...
Forget that pussy willow! Let him go.
You went too far, Kaito!
This is hardly the outcome we need to...
I know that, man!

And I know that sometimes, it comes down to more than just logic.
But you see...
No matter how determined you are, there's still a difference between *bravery* and *recklessness!!*
The whole thing's pointless if he gets himself killed!!
......
You're right. I'd forgotten that you...well...

Will you clean up your act, Todoroki?
I told you to capture the Category Zero.
What's the big deal?
It doesn't change the end result—we're gonna kill them right here.

Don't glare at me like that...
Okay, fine. I'll do as you say.
You don't have to remind me. I'll kill him, all right.

...Just not right away.

The more time I spend watching her, the cuter she looks.
I can sure tell why he loves her so much.

Bit by bit...
Piece by piece...
...I'll steal everything he holds dear.
And when he's wallowing in despair and solitude, I'll swoop in for the kill.

Ack!

SPSHH
Rrgh!

......

SPLOSH
SPLOSH

What's wrong with me?
What am I doing...?

You're supposed to save the world, *remember?!*
Of course I do...

But...
How do I beat that guy...?

FZZT

FWOOM
Aaah!!

How's that? A little drier?
Huh?

Kaito...
THUD
ドスッ
You didn't dry it, you *burned* it.
Ha ha! Sorry, sorry.

......

SCRITCH
ポリ
SCRITCH
ポリ
......
......

Does that still hurt?
On your cheek.
Huh?

......
Yeah...

Well, I ain't apologizin' for it.
Yeah...

What?
Just shut up and listen!
Oh, okay...
There were a brother and sister who lived in a Nationless Quarter—er, I mean, lawless area.
Their dad and mom had died in a car crash...
...And they bounced around between unsympathetic relatives until they arrived at this place.
It was a dangerous town.
Drugs, robberies, murders, you name it... You had to be strong to survive.
東亞泊
So the older brother pledged to be strong.
He believed that if he was strong, he could provide for and protect his little sister.

Soon, the brother was the toughest guy in the entire town.
He made many friends, and got even tougher, so he could watch out for them, too.
His sister said, "Stop doing all these dangerous things."
She was probably worried be- cause from her perspective, it *was* dangerous stuff he was up to.
Then, the sister was kid- napped.
It was survival of the fittest. Whoever shows their weakness, loses.
The brother snapped, and charged in by himself, without thinking.
In the end, he was helpless against many. He was crushed.
And on top of that, the sister died to protect her own stupid brother, the one who was supposed to be watching out for her...
That's the end of the story.
Is...

Listen.
SHH
If you die, that's the end of it.
If you die, who's going to save Ayano?

If you die...
ZSHH
...Every-thing is meaning-less!!
SPSH
SPSH

Aww, crap.
Only two skips, that time.
I'm losing my edge...
Let's head back.
We've got to come up with a plan so we can save Ayano, on the double.

Ain't that right, Kakeru?
......
......
BUMP
Yeah!

!?
......
What's up?

Ripples?
What about 'em?
......

!!

I have to go...to the Green-house.
Come on, man... What did I just say?
I figured it out.
Figured what out?
The way to beat Todoroki!!

DSHH
I did it...
I did it!!
HUFF
HUFF
I can face off against him with this!
I might even be able to save Ayano!!
Kakeru!
Kakeru!!
I can practically hear Ayano calling for me now!

THWAM
Listen up, everyone!!

!!
Wha...?

?
What's wrong? Why are you so shocked...?

Right... To the right!
On your... shoulder...

?
My right... shoulder?

......
Whaaaaaa-?!
H-hello?
Ayano?!

When the guy appeared before me and Kakeru...
Aren't you cute? You should be my girl.
ZZIP
It was immediately obvious that he was a psychic.
I want to make you mine... by force!!
VWEEB
Whaaa...
SWOOP
THUD
The next thing I knew, I was in the midst of a thick forest.
Where... am I?
Kakeru...
As my consciousness slowly ebbed away, I attempted to project myself...
nd that
eated...

Meeee!

Are you surprised? Huh?

Hmm...

Well, Kakeru, why don't you show us your plan for defeating Todoroki?
Come on, look over here! Look at me!

Okay, jokes aside—I was *not* expecting this.
I've never seen this before.
This must have something to do with Ayano's powers of telepathy and astral projection.
Maybe it's some strange combination of the two.

Perhaps she lost consciousness during the act of projection...
Ouch!
...and the piece of her mind that was being projected was cut off and made independent.

So is it one of those ghostly *residual imprint* things, or what?
KSHH
Not exactly, but close enough.
KSHH
Look! Look here!
POING
I put a ribbon on him!
Whee!
Hee hee!

Shut... upppppp!!
Try to be at least a tiny bit serious, can't you?!
Isn't she the one we're all worried about?!
Why is she the least con-cerned of all of us?!
Scary!
It might be a bit different from the Ayano we know, but it's still a piece of her.
This is quite good news, actually.
Why?
It means that as long as this Ayano is still here, we know she's all right.

And the fact that we haven't heard from Ayano's telepathy means she's currently unable to use her powers.
If she *was* able to use them, she could probably escape using her projection.
And there's only *one* place with the psychic cancelling tools to prevent her from doing so...
Which means Ikushima and his pals must be in the Greenhouse.

We should still have time...
So tell us, Kakeru.
How can we beat Todoroki?

...Are you kidding...?
And this is going to work...?

Well, there is a logic to it...
How can it *possibly* succeed?!

I don't know.
But you were right, Kaito. If I go there right now, I'll only get myself killed.

There's a key to beating Todoroki.

All I want...
...is just a little bit of time.

...You got it.
Let's trust in Kakeru.

Well...
I'll be back!
BAM
WORLD
PERFECT

Kakeru!!
Huh?
Wha-!
Ayano?!
SWISH
はしっ
SMOOCH
チュッ
Ayano!
BOINK
ぴょん
Make it quick.
Come and save me!

On the inside, Ayano's scared...
You bet!
ZFF
He's gone.
Sure is.
As for the rest of us...
We'll just have to wait until he gets back.

Big trouble, people!
THWAM
Hiyama-san!
What's the matter? You're all out of breath.
Just come outside and see!
ZMMM

Wh...
What *is* this...?

This is crazy...
The entire town...

...is surrounded...
...by some giant "wall" thing...

It's no good...
It won't budge an inch!
FSSS

When did this show up, Hiyama-san?!
I don't know! I left to go buy some groceries, and there it was.
What's going on, Jôi?!
Well...
SHH...
It's a "time wall."
A time wall?!
What the hell is *that*?!
The time in here, and the time beyond the wall...
...are starting to drift apart.

You don't mean...
The *time*...?
There's a psychic that can *do* that?
Exactly.
It is the price of Kakeru's Chronodiver ability...
The little distortions that occur when cutting and pasting the film we call the world.
At first, it might just be fractions of a second...
But when it stretches to several sec-onds...several minutes...the world no longer exists as one.

But this is too early! With the amounts Kakeru was shifting, it shouldn't have reached this point, yet.
Then how...?
Remember?
There's *another* psychic who shares Kakeru's power.

I should have expected this!
WHAM
I should have realized it was possible, when I knew they both had the same power!
Let's go.
Where?
To the Greenhouse.
We have to stop Ikushima!

B-but what about Kakeru?
We don't have time! Every second counts, now.
We have to do everything we can to slow them down until Kakeru returns...
Or else everything is lost!!
......

That's right.
Well, that makes things simple, doesn't it?
We should have just done this from the start.
HMMM
ぼーっ
....
Me, too!
You have to guard the school.
Awww!!
Just tell Kakeru what happened, if he comes back!
Until then, enjoy being the damsel in distress.
Don't worry. Kakeru and the rest of us will save you.
Please...
Here we go.

HFFF
I know you're there! Come on out!
If you don't, I'll use my powers!
You know how I'm not supposed to waste them on trivial things!
Come on out, before I blow up the world, or something!

Tomoe-chaaan!!
Where are youuu?!

CRIKK

GSHHAA

Oh, brother.
I feel sorry for the people in your world if they get destroyed over something like *that.*
...What did I tell you?
Huh?
T... Tomoe-chan?
You can see me whenever you want, so long as you wish for it...
What?! Really?
Yes... So what is it?
......
I...

At this point, having more power isn't going to help you.

Huh...?
I'm not saying that you can't beat your problem.
You've noticed it, too, haven't you?
You can't beat Todoroki with the way you're *using* your power.
And you don't know how you *ought* to be using it.
That's why you're here.

NOD

But I'm not God...
If I could just power you up with a flick of the wrist, I'd have done it already.
You can't just run to me...
...and expect all of your problems to be solved.
Awww.
......

By the way, things have been rather wild outside. Are you sure you want to be whiling away the time in here?
Huh?
What, you didn't know?
FLIK
Look at this.

Gasp... It's the gang!

But why...
Why are they at the Green-house?

Wait... What's with that huge wall?!
What's happening to our town?!

It's a time distortion... A wall of time.
It would seem the end is nigh.
A...time wall?
That's right. A reaction to your psychic power.
But in this case, it's responding to the *other* one's usage...
T-this is bad...
Sorry, Tomoe-chan! Send me back! I need to meet up with the others!
I can't do that.

GWW
Huh...?
!?
Aaah!!
DWOMMM

......
Tomoe-chan...
What was *that* for?!
I-I could have *died!!*
That wasn't very funny, you know!
That's because it wasn't a joke.
Huh?
I was actually trying to kill you.

DOBOOM
GSHH
DMMM
But why?!
THWAP
GWOOMM

ZWOO
ZSHH
Aaaagh!!
...Huh?
Nothing happened...
Geez, what's the big idea? You scared me!
...
This is really going too far! I'm mad, now!

Aaaahhh!!
!!
My hand...
It's all wrinkled... But why...?
This sword cannot cut a person in two.
Huh?
But it *does* greatly speed up the aging process of your cells.
Take one too many hits, and you'll shrivel up into an old man and die.

Throw a force at him equal to what he is using, and you nullify his effects.

50 50

But to achieve that, it will require precise control of your ability.

That is what you truly need now.
So make your choice, boy.
You cannot leave without defeating me.

In order to escape, you will have to best me, or die.

To be continued in volume 6

Psycho Busters

Omake 4-Panel Manga
Daily
Psycho
Busters

Lining Up

Wow, this place sure is packed...
Y-you said it...
Akihabara

Look at that, Kakeru! What a line!
Really? I wonder what it's for. A new game, I bet.
GRMM GRMM
New Dating Sim Sale Line

What the-?!

Hey, there's a street singer! Wow, Akihabara's just *full* of surprises!
K... Kaito-san?!

Gamer

Puberty 3

STAFF: Yûya Aoki
Akinari Nao
Tatsu Nakajima
Naoto Shinoda
Kiyomizu
Subaru Matsuyama
SPECIAL THANKS:
Keitarô Yanagibashi

Translation Notes

Japanese is a tricky language for most Westerners, and translation is often more an art than a science. For your edification and reading pleasure, here are notes on some of the places where we could have gone in a different direction, or where a Japanese cultural reference is used.

Okonomiyaki, page 8

Okonomiyaki is a Japanese dish originating from the Kansai (Western Japan) area around Ôsaka and Kyôto. Literally meaning "cook what you like," it is made by pouring a special batter onto a griddle and then sprinkling various savory toppings over it, such as meat, vegetables and shrimp. In *okonomiyaki* restaurants, the customers are given a bowl of ingredients at a special table with a hot-plate, so they can cook it themselves with the toppings they like (hence the name). Due to the appearance and preparation, it is sometimes introduced outside of Japan as "Japanese pizza" or "Japanese pancakes." *Okonomiyaki* sauce is very thick and sweet.

Sobameshi, page 8

Sobameshi is a combination of *yakisoba* (Japanese chow mein) and rice. Though rarely served together, this is one case where noodles and rice are combined into one dish. The toppings of pork, cabbage and onions make it taste similar to *okonomiyaki*, even if the texture is quite different.

Akihabara, page 51

Akihabara, also known by the nickname of "Akiba," is a neighborhood in Tokyo with a heavy number of electronics and gaming stores. It's a mecca of sorts to all types of nerds and *otaku*, whether it's videogaming, electronics, anime—you name it, you can find it there.

Maid café, page 52

Cafés and coffee shops are a common sight around Japan, but one particular category that is rising in popularity in recent years is the maid café. Maid cafés take advantage of the popular maid trend in anime/manga by hiring cute waitresses to dress in maid's clothing (as seen here) and call the customers "Master." Because of the *otaku* angle, most maid cafés are found in areas like Akihabara.

Oden, page 55

Oden is a type of hodgepodge stew with a variety of ingredients such as boiled eggs, *daikon* radishes, fish cakes, tofu, octopus, and many others. It's a winter dish and is usually cooked and served in a big pot, so eating it out of a can is a rather unorthodox means of enjoying it.

Psycho Busters, Volume 6 Preview

We're pleased to present you with a preview from volume 6. Please check the Del Rey website for information on when this volume will be released in English. For now, though, you'll have to make do with Japanese!

なーんて♡

ぐあ!?
ボクを そこらの
サイキックと一緒にして
もらっちゃ困るなぁ
そんな‥‥
一体何が起きたって
いうの‥‥?
テメーらとは
格がちげーんだよ

まぁ 少しは
楽しめたよ
お礼に
さっきと同じことを
してあげよう
ペチャンコに
なって 死ね
‥‥やめて‥‥

……!!
……?
何ともない……?

遅れてごめん

カケル!!
もう僕は
迷わない……!!

TOMARE!

[STOP!]

You're going the wrong way!

Manga is a completely different type of reading experience.

To start at the *beginning*, go to the *end*!

That's right! Authentic manga is read the traditional Japanese way—from right to left, exactly the *opposite* of how American books are read. It's easy to follow: Just go to the other end of the book, and read each page—and each panel—from right side to left side, starting at the top right. Now you're experiencing manga as it was meant to be!